A SONG AT TWILIGHT

A SONG AT TWILIGHT
JIM DINE

CUNEIFORM PRESS

ISBN: 978-1-950055-03-6

Distributed by:
Small Press Distribution
1341 Seventh Street
Berkeley, CA 94710-1409
Tel. (800) 869-7553
www.spdbooks.org

Published by Cuneiform Press
www.cuneiformpress.com

for Asa Benveniste
1925–1990
"Foolish enough to have been a poet"

CONTENTS

Jewish Fate

As they say, Jewish Fate

That's the title, "Jewish Fate."

Drunk on the Holy Spirit

Drunk on the Holy Spirit

Polaroids, chromogenics, gelatin silver prints

Diana and I talking about Mark Hampton's description of her fingers.

She's wearing her red shawl.

Jewish fate.

I think something else happens were I to be from it.

My big exuberance is the curse of the positive.

I don't always know about the moment.

The power—

Being human at sunset

Vibrates back, lit, and this and this

So isolated.

So violated.

A plan to pay me back involving refinancing and I must give a mere one hundred thousand dollars to tide you over, as they say, 'til the next tide of debt and fear.

You can go to jail, you know, or me or with me.

Leon's store sold plumbing supplies and tools and toilets and sinks and all kinds of little stuff like washers and nails and light bulbs.

So easy the dream

Falling toward Zion.

Always correcting and reinventing the drawing.

With you it is now, it's refinancing and the threat of paying the dollars and in a few minutes the months go by, and I know this isn't what you want.

But taxes and refinancing

The photograph of your huge shadow distinct in its hatred of goodwill and trust.

The fast payback.

A better footing for the dark shadow of the giant.

Never release me.

Don't ever. Thank you, for never releasing me.

I worked there every Saturday and every summer for ten years beginning when I was nine. They got me to sort little stuff that had been ordered to replace what had been sold. Barrels of nails needed to be opened with a steel nail claw. A metal hand really. I would put the different sizes into empty wooden bins.

From this girdle that surrounds the house, that surrounds your stomach, your hips, the formal garden, surrounding the house, the razor, the tools, the thousands of dollars shine.

On the wheels of young girls, on their leaves, their technique.

I am the willing model. It's easier to look at me than to view a stranger.

It is also possible to make me sad in my shoes with the vitriol of debt that you drown in like your lies in the jam pot, my friend, in front of the Christmas Tree.

It was very boring but it gave me time when I was nine to daydream among objects about the beauty of the white glaze on the bathroom fixtures for instance. There were paint color charts and beautiful big red bolt cutters that eventually twenty years later entered my drawings as a man.

This is all to give you the atmosphere of the place. I really want to talk about two men I worked with there who eventually, when I was fourteen, I worked for helping them load and unload trucks that came with supplies to sell and trucks taking away orders of kitchens or very heavy supplies, cast iron sewer pipe to a contractor who was building a house.

This is the picture I want.

This is the picture I want.

A debt to the work, but the work from the River Styx, mania dear, plus, and then, sleeping opposite hours. You're asleep, I'm awake, smiling, etc., the hooligan touching the blue wind, fingers, toes gone, but feet, little feet gone.

You stayed home and did not come. Your shadow was gray and small then. But in 1968, these images were trusting and the cake was very slightly taken care of.

TERRIBLE!

He's good to me. He doesn't tell me who I am. The snapshots are very focused on the picture. Not the hours and the years of trusting. The mammoth's shadow looms over the hilarious.

Joe Kibbing. Joe Kibbing was about six foot three and very thin. He was of German descent. He had been born, like my father, in Covington, Kentucky, across the Ohio River from us. He starred at a Catholic High School as a basketball player. After the army, he went to work at Mr. Morris' store. Mr. Morris was Morris Cohen, my grandfather, and owner of the store with his son. Joe was very dramatic and high strung and didn't take orders easily. And energy. Many years of energy. And scheming.

And your violence of embezzlement.

I worked there every Saturday, every summer for ten years. When I was nine, they got me to sort little stuff.

Loom over the hilarious.

High-strung and don't take orders easily.

And energy. Many years of energy.

The mélange of pain. The etchings, drawings, sculpture of my time. The paint, my heart, my brushes, my nerve ends never hear the hand in my pocket. Your hand in my pocket. The watch on my wrist so far away. The dragon sits with the devil on his shadow. Language is clear.

Joe's older brother, who we all called "Bud," his real name Marcellis, was the head salesman at the store. He came to work there as soon as World War II ended and never left, a soft-spoken, intelligent man who, had he had an education past High School, might have been a lawyer or a surgeon. He was the older brother and very dignified.

Back to Joe.

Joe was stressed. He felt stressed by every order he was given. Plus he had a problem with hemorrhoids so there was sometimes blood on the seat of his khaki wash pants.

Intense and dark so that's not good enough to photograph the crib.

It looks dark, too.

What's cremating about that?

Why people are not very interested in?

Your job's making the big shadow to look over the girl's shoulder.

Life's ass.

A good bite.

You are nice and terrifying. I embarrass nice people. You were nice too and scary. The fullness of me in the Holy City. Chanson de Noël.

Chanson de Noël.
Chanson de Noël.
Chanson de Noël.

Look now, a complete mirage. The Holy City, the perfect carnage, and you lay blame on my feelings and not on your lying fingers in the black back pocket of the old warrior.

Joe of course worked right through the hemorrhoids. No one mentioned it to him because how could you then? But for me it was a mystery that held my eyes, this blood suddenly appearing and no one asking about it. Anyway, he was the head shipping clerk.

But the feet, the little feet are gone.

The hooligan poverty.

The rhythm of the rag. Oh rag. Oh southern uncle. Do the spit. Do the money lender.

There was a man he worked with called Willie Tapp. Willie was younger than Joe so when I met him, he was probably twenty-two. He had been a track star in High School, and quit, came to work at this store. He was short and lithe. I could see how fast he must have been in the dashes.

Claude Poussin up on the Janiculum. They try to invent.

Not aligning a magic landscape.

We had Rome for a minute in a mirror, an accurate difference in a world of drawing. My eyes, my eye, my eye now tearing, now tearing and sad for the years I was blind to the shadow of your objects.

Tapp, he dressed elegantly like a lot of black guys did then for a guy loading trucks and handling greasy tools and heavy boxes. He was very zoot suit, pegged pants and always a fancy shirt. He was a desperate alcoholic and reeked of cheap whiskey. This handsome, lovely man showed up for work drunk on Saturday, but managed to perform most times. I saw Mr. Morris send him home when he couldn't walk, but he was a jive artist and he hid his high fairly well.

Tapp called Morris' son Leon, his "lopsided cousin." I said, "Why Tapp? Why do you call him your lop-sided cousin?" He said, "Because his wallet's in the back right pocket and it's so full of money it made him lopsided."

Like an alchemist

Geppetto bites the talking stick.

Love and grief.

Christ and Venus.

I thought this was great.

Mr. Lopside was a mean fool anyway.

Cracks in the shadow.

Bleeding in the vein.

I hear it.

I hear it. It's an image, the sculpture, as an image, that's what I mean.

Christ and Venus. He is the man. She's gone to Japan.

Three ex-votos do their job. She's gone to Japan with Hadrian holding himself like the man who carved him.

I went to blow glass. Ex-votos from red dye and sand. Cracks that will move and bleed like bleeding veins eventually. To dream among the votive objects, arranged by chance in beauty, your birth, the rebirth of the familiar face and a sense of fun and fear at finding things she most cared about removed as liquid waste.

Chainsaw, a chainsaw, dear old friend on top of the world. The dust from the cuts. The foot-long log, kicking back at my face. Feral, feral, razor, tools, the dollars shine on the wheel. Carved with a chainsaw, cast in bronze, painted with lead, glazed over with black, the palm of my hand like ink on the wood cut.

The dust from the cuts. The six-foot long log kicking back at my face.

As if it were the first time, each person so nice, so unique in that year, open to spending and bringing a narcissistic brain to my pocket. Kicking back at my face.

My Letter to the Troops

Who was
George? George,
Who was always so eager
To make everyone feel welcome.
He broke his dish when I dropped mine.
He learns of Blind Pew at the Admiral Benbow and Jim Hawkins being George
he thought the second war was a sanctuary of fellows.
"Not so," said the Cyclops.
His anger at everything was shining and made old
By one eye's sadness, the ether, the knife, the fictional home.

I've checked the day light
The drops of blood, work my big toe on my right foot, asleep on the next toe,
resting.
Your savior obsession—the mass,
The civil privileges given us by you
The "false" foot, <u>forward</u> on
Our property, the orange robe visits
With our other preferences
Like the hair,
Rubbed off the beard
Against the tree on the veld,
The head,
Wrinkled by age
Fat
As ever—Back to Front
With an angel arriving and untangling those gone.

Eunice is gone,
Dead, dead, dead
Fred's dead,
Hercules died without me, Chloe too
Ernie Donagh dead... and now
And now
Doc's gone.

In between the delivery room in the hospital and the new brick house on Cheyenne
Drive I lived with my Grandma and Grandpa on the North Crescent. They lived in a
small house like their neighbors. There were a few very grand places but they were hard
to imagine as I was one and two years old. Grandma's floors were very polished and
there was a small stain glass on the way upstairs. My mother and I slept in one of the
3 bedrooms. There was also an attic but I was too afraid to look in it. Our bathroom

smelled of old folks. It was tiled white with black tesserae for accent and the toothbrush-es lying around had lost their hair. In the basement was my grandpa's wizard table where he did his sleight-of-hand thinking. His hammer held the most power and the noise it made when it struck a nail or for that matter any surface amplified the random anger swimming around there from his porcine fist.

I have raised the ongoing tension question.
Stepping up the alert status.
I seek your understanding.
I am affected by the access, in and out.
We are mothering relevant governments and military watercolors are vibrant and at attention.
The girl,
The angel,
The Rembrandt portrait of defection, exhaling clouds of life into the cold air.
I feel love, really up there inside you/"new appearances."
"Where's that?" She asked,
America?

America is marching in an unlikely manner.
1000 lines of battle
2 feathers
Come to
Camp ground.
Mr. and Mrs. Full up
Upstairs coyotes. Unfaithful
Coyotes, cougars
Wheat fields, unfaithful
Apple trees on the
Side of the Jerusalem hills. unfaithful
5 year old fingers
Unfaithful and—
Faithful.
And unfaithful wives, husbands,
The landscape, unfaithful,
Friends and cousins,
My grandchildren.
The neighbors across the road (and their animals)
Your plants
The people who tend your plants,
Unfaithful.

Voice, the answer, the moon.
The crook of my arm/moves the flesh,
The blue desert, to no effect
High and verdant

Animals are chilling your lavender
Is fading to lavender.
Please send me home/to the edge of the evening,
The Blood moon,
You miss it and
October will crowd itself to no effect.

Speak "The Joseph Poem."
The Shining Bed with phallus
It turns to dust
A Son of God appears
"A gold baby"
(The audience witnesses the birth.)
The proprietor,
An old guy wearing his own conversation like a regular customer looks at
The radio, very loud in the middle of the night or is it tomorrow night
killing the session,
A mark of an unlikely messenger
Knowing the website of the government's channels.
The ongoing development between northern and southern property owners.
They try to be aware of
"Top-Man."
The deep purple reflex
His bouquet of juniper bares witness to the soldiers
Well-knit by the lies of autumn.

Styria,
Once again its
Complex soil is—
A vagina of money.
The expression of rage, blessed soul and screaming tenor,
Listening to the impulse of strokes
The history of screams—
Bernini,
Damaged by a crack
Executed and invented by memory
Shaping the new Christian road block.

Bring me my charcoal sticks!
I must draw the Popes
The bust of the Popes.
Urban
Paul
Reuben
John
Francis, I must make

Their blurred faces
A mark on the paper
The buildup of carbon on my palms.
On my palms.

Who was George?
North of the Villa Borghese?
George,
Where Pope Julius lived in a leafy green room
George,
Who was always so eager for his orange trees.
To make everyone feel welcome in his quiet haven.
He broke his dish when I dropped mine.
I paid my entrance fee.
George learns of Blind Pew at the Admiral Benbow.
His Jewish classics, like the Pantheon for instance,
Were so sure the second war was a sanctuary of fellows.
"Not so," said the Cyclops.
It is full of pain and his anger
Everything was shining and made old
By "one eye's" sadness, the ether and the knife.
A Ghetto tradition
Slightly scorched around the edges.
George, to avoid competition, fills the cavities with nuts
And his sense of terror, a medical falsehood.
George, you're a brave man
On the next toe
You've been a lot of places
Your savior obsession—the dark section doesn't hold
The civil privileges
You might find on any peoples telephone
"Us by you kid"—
Did the cab come or stand on your "false" foot forward
How about a little light on our own property, Tonight
A rebuke,
("Do you think you're being too Chinese?")
This is a perception of pirates giving me the black spot
By the Creator.
Privacy, a coming of age word
My sea chest, stolen by my relative or
Some local acquaintance
Who empties my house of
Sacred objects that I owned
And was able to buy
Because of the gifts in my left hand.
All your purses on the bed

Clawed at by the children
Owned by them now
So meaningless
The robbery of my heart
Two thieves and the victims
All swimming in our tears
Caressed by gold
And foundry costs.
In front of our eyes
The boy removes
The hot ore
There is little left now
To steal
In America, marching and
Eating as fast as we can
Japan, winning the contest.

So my brother won't leave his room
Broken and sure of his comb over
A martian's waffle
Bacon and sovereign freedom;
Safe and waiting for
Papal rule.
Eggs and pancakes
No death penalty!
Moths carry me along through the moon's glow.
Pale and sweating,
Stealing your flutter and your carnal smile.

I've become a tramp
My daughter
I smell you through my aching knees.
In the sweet bye and bye
The fear of passion is
Hard to sustain.
The music of the Virgin's touch,
Is more like Jesus and then,
The earth starts to dread the star
Missing you.
I really should try "loneliness."
I called to say;
Breakfast was great and forgive me for being old.
The wild family, meanwhile,
Will tell me that the trees grow wild again,
Over,
Us... on top of us.

Happy.
Anew.
The parrot at sunrise.
My ferocious image
And winter's breath.
3:00 a.m.
Two Venus' on Kozo paper—
In me.
I'm me, thanks to the loss of labor
And systemic sprays.
Our entrée
To completely missing the point about,
What this poem is about.
Our imperfect life
But our life and age/
That's what counts.
Replacing
The sewer pipes
In our town
Underground
New deep holes
Rooted in a very real landscape
The place beyond the words
A slight,
Clear,
Ravishing voice
Is a hopeless hazard.
The moon fills the silent house
Earth gives birth to time
And heaven is a jealous
Parliament.
The mad dog is swimming
In the icy waters,
Not having any idea
About the mysterious
Temperature of age.
Home is where
Bugs crawl on our heads
At night
After you hit the floor like a barber pole
A black abstraction
Whispering across
The history of
Color.
This week I painted, painted, painted
The possibility

Of permanent silence.
Well... it could
Happen even though
I am so happy
Trying to hold the tightness
Of this celebration of
Neighbors.
This family
Understanding how paper
Can undulate,
I kiss you.
I hear the Indian waters
In my fingers.
The Boatman's Confession
Is a mysterious boulevard.
It brings you soft slain
To my voice
Leaning back,
On the front seat of the truck
Down a long green street
There's an exit
By your ankles.
Fabulous!
Barking at stones
A blind futile event in my
Mind.
A light in my resident body,
Walks the halls of world issues
On the side panel.
"Beautiful Canada"
Sitting in this country
I smell your hair, your scalp,
The last time
It was Pep's before she was gone/
The magnificent break
Of arteries
And the road to blood

We live forever
On a minute
With the ghost of love.
The Rose of Sharon
Is in full bloom here
The air is fecund with her odor,
And why not?
The art of age

The art of age

Am I blue, Am I blue
These tears in my eyes
Telling you.
How kind god was to the sculptor
So kiss him again
How can you ask me
Am I blue ?
The break is perfect
The alarm clock, a visiting zanax
The whole point is delicacy
A sign of its pale color
Tenderness
Of the new apricot buds
The sudden appearance of little fruit
Fuel for the painter
The dream blossom of a long ago garden
Bland, in the old positive sense "suave"

This is a dear life!

Nantes

The beheading / The beheading of Palmyra
Too early to wake the dog, but—
The soldier enters
The De Chirico room.
Room smells of rooms.
The patina of children
Room smells of children's
clothes—
the unfaithful ground cover.
Joan Mitchell's
clothes—
Blot the paint
with them!
Mother, gone—
Blot the paint
The carpenter comes into
the room—with
mosquitoes & traffic
Sound
the clarion!
old beast—
Enter the fort /
Visit the childhood!
no beheading but—
There is sadness
about the body—
Rip the door from the
jamb Coyote!
cry! scream!
smell
the children!
Clarion rings for
common
prayer—
matins,
never
mother—
Bullets jump around
the bed—
Coyote screams with no warning!
——————————

"I was only looking

out the window at
nothing but light
in the field at autumn"
said I, Numb
I am alarmed to
discover I have
stopped noticing
the crimes around
us.
My body wants to
be alone
when
"it really is
alone."
this is an orgy of
anonymous guys,
mocking the people
who are capable
of ecstatic encounters
I am alarmed to
discover
I have faith in
THIS, in THIS
AND—this / and—
The Secret Drawings
the line of black
ink soup,
The shocking pink
Flamingos,
The cold
bananas, eat
them like candy.
Smiling they die—
in the parrot jungle,
The voice of the
Seminole
wrestles with
dreamers /
alligators,
Sluggish from
the salt mud
enter the room.

Harriet Baeker
among the many young
Norwegian artists

of promise
paints her intimacy
onto the carpet.
Mary Magdalen alone
at the winter
corrida.
Her red brain
far from the
"windows
of dark love",
The name in
cement—
written.

The SAMURAI again
folks—
He is transforming the
room, just by
Standing
He gets a little
nervous
by the late gifts
of light... and... and...
poetry
The attitude of
his legs—
not the strength of them
They are old.
You have the legs
of a dancer old
Soldier—(pause)
I need some years still.
I am happy to he
a prisoner of my
ageless
emotions.
There is a whole
sky of ultramarine
blue as
the water
stains the paper.
Venus is drawing
and Apollo sings
like Orpheus.
The sirens
push the foot to change

I call and wish
every one
"Buona notte"
Icarus is
with me. (By the way)
My legs,—
have the muscles /
of a young monkey
The scans of
this house of words
sing the songs
of this soaring embrace.
I hug the screen.
mon chéri,
I am a defiant
Miner
I tremble
for color Trying to be a pensioner /
my ageless emotions
are once again
unfaithful ground cover
ah the radiance of blame.
BLOT THE PAINT JOAN!!
use your skirt—
Blot the paint!
Lets go!
"Have you noticed—
The Fado is like a
raga"
Let the sunlight in.
What I can see of
the street is empty
I find myself
wondering
if I were to be
arrested and
didn't come back
what would I do?
I guess I would go home and demand
my release /
"I suppose"
from these women who
fade away
in
Vienna,
Matisse,

Chinese food,
old tools, this
red hot *piment*!!
the lentils could bring
good fortune and
the light from the
moon around my
head is illuminated
by the SAW)—
while I whistle
and try to hit high notes
and still be
on key.
your half of
paradise
makes the sea bright
and I lay down my
Sword and Shield /
That convict,
That crook, that lost
interest
in rain and
Heaven.
Black cherries in mourning
for flamingos
stained by radiance.
in Dixie,
Burn the angel with her rose.
the sun
limits a bitter sweet
bounce,
while white doves
sing
Handel
and I think of
you
and your
being here
alone.
OK?

(then double
bass plays
1st 16 bars
of Barbara
song—"NANTES")

The wall in Brézin (for O.B.)

Block my entrance, we know
the rude way
I am treated by women.
Jealous of their age
older than me, even,
and I want nothing to cry about
till the end of...
Block my way—
I pray for Cardinal Lustiger!
not the ice cream pope
not the zinnias
or the cosmos,
so for 2 years
I spend each evening
in the cathedral
with the Chinese
and the Serbians
and of course,
the Irish women block my way.
I wrench the earth
where we were / your ashes
from the sea to the salt marsh,
The Great Lake
Behind the apple trees.
I think of the old Hudson
a river for your wheels, 90 year old
baby, abstract to speak
like a big boy
not like a radio child
or your heart like a truck
not confident about praise
and obscurity.
Is this a poem about love?
Is the committee
taking a census?
is this a love poem ?
I REMEMBER

The Answer

Innocence
and sleep
there is a sad
embrace
as we cheat the carpenter.
Please wrap my arms in white cloth.
They are cold
       keep me awake
       like my dreams /
I wake up /
my ears,
go red.
the answer

Printing in Austria (for V.B.)

circulating air
softer than
my suicide
or the whiskey on
the pillows / thinking
about abstraction.
The big one is
very comic too!
kill someone at random /
a remote signal, the immaculate door
true as Paris Pants,
they stop
and go
disappearing women.
          singing, stop, go, looking
leave.

Bon à tirer

Crevasse in the forehead
wrinkles from intaglio
The sun is rational and the
the wrinkles tell the
poems,
Don't sleep
            on La Plata.
Between the buttons,
did God
fix it so it can't happen ?
even though,
you live with the nettles

Defenestration & tacking

Horace meets OVID and
names the North Star "Brilliant"
The point is the time traveler
is looking past the guide
to unlimited sleep
True comfort like no other—
The STAR is the class of all
positions in the air.
This last love of
the famous
simply followed her nose
out the window.
a prime act and
an encore of place,
geographically.
Name the quiet emotion
that over takes me.
look at it carefully and silently
Herod,
harem pants
laurel wreath and
loose coat
made of shiny chintz
          bright pink.
turned up slippers
big shirt with floral print
Kurtah ?
big belt
my stomach showing off.

Esso

on <u>Sunday</u>—out for a
      service check
      Monday—serve Anna Maria
      and Lopez the same
      if not later
as I'm in Montrouge now.
Le concert de ce soir
est un on the Rue Madame
on Monday, the anxiety
of Munich——
      a hundred a week
      as long as it lasts—
The pepper in your corner
the dollars in the money bowl
The hall where you cannot
even keep the 6 pence—
But,
It's my style to leave cash
lying around

Voyage to the coast

I am a potato chip
       from
the pepper, who eats at me /
Dear Boy,
Who builds my work for the jumping ?
we drive and
The water is at my waist.
I am pulled with the
       coroner /
          was it on purpose
          or an accident
          in the garden
I see the rosemary
       bloom for fun
certainly without sun and wind
and now the salt
is gone from
the chips

Birthday Greetings

BEST VIENNESE SPRING IN,
    76 YEARS, SINCE BEAUTY
    NEVER LEAVES YOU /
    LIKE THE HONEY
    FOUND IN EGYPT
THERE IS STILL SWEETNESS
    AND COLOR,
IN YOUR EYE
AND THE ART
YOU BEAR.

Church Nights

The SISTERS—
giggles and OOHS
      Fawned and awe
      over the Jew Poet.
The one
was asked
for an endorsement...
The OLD boy's book
NO,
That's impossible Jimmy—
He "OBJECTIFIES" women!
Like Morandi
with his vessels
or the late Ted B.
      and Bob C.
————————————————

"ANNE-THE-WORLD"
in all the places to go
in my 70's travel log
My private jokes
the humorless (When do i get my copy)
GENTILES /
surrounding, the
People's house of worship
THAT lives in the device
I built
to hold the tool.
For a full week,
a clot
for a full week
Among others.
Hard as a knot you ate,
you hate,
The blood is in it

So Long...

Then the power
sunk into
the autumn
and we had no time

The Dog

as i attack
the vise
that holds
the copper
tubing to be
cut—
half
of my index finger
remains
in my grinder

Health & Sunshine

Have love, and confidence in your body
Today, remembering love
old and believable
your whole self protected.
by the sun / bigger than ever,
I cannot resist you / to life!
Don't be afraid of the iron foot
I promise
as i pick the black olives out of the bread.
I thought of your big feeling
for yourself
for me <u>and</u>
the waiter,
thinks I'm nuts because there
is a pile of mutilated bread on the
table without olives
who cares ? Who's ever caring
The Nazis ?
The castrated staff of life ?
The holy see ?

Saint-Christophe, La Baule

Do you think Japan
will ever serve
you at the Cafe Flore ?
Is Harry really
dead after his oeuf plat ?
and where is
Jules and Pierre
and Samy the
old car mechanic
with white aprons ?
Get seeds at
Vilmorin!

get big pot for
avocado and earth
& fertilizer for avocado
go G20
milk   crackers
coffee   musili
eggs   oranges
butter   bananas
salami   onions
tomatoes—   patrimony
Ancestral patrimony.
Go madame

visit plants

go Brézin

begin clean

up start

poem (big)

called

BEAUTY IS LONESOME

BEAUTY IS LONELY

really start

Jewish fate

trilogy

try to write

about 2 weeks

with the fairy princes.

My fear at

the rules she

laid down. How

strange her face

Sleep is a bit

lonely like

beauty

and the

art of painting

TOV

at the gym
one of her
feet is at
3 o'clock
the other
at 9:00 A.M.
it is brand
new
sucking water
for electricity,
the small of the
back
a darker grey
me biking
to Byzantium
and what ?
close my
eyes ?
I could lose
my way
amongst
the crumbs
the path
to youth
the hair
in your armpits
Queen Christina
now a grandma
deaf to jokes
about her DNA
under her
nails
the lamps
of the Buddha
that are all, not sure here,
forgetting
smile and
the dead
virus
washes away
every so often,
a fact

about
making
noses
smaller
and the
memory
of you in
the barnyard
Oh, how the
earth does
sing now
that her
feet
are at
8 and 2:00
and much
more
limber

_____

a free ride

from lower
saxony
to goulash
with pork,
Herr Szabo
is jolly and
out-of-sorts
with the state
that brings
students to
mull over
the
economy.
meine Landsmann!
We distrust
the runners
and the
strummers.
so giddy up (in the)
Schwartzwald.
a dry rotten
city
often called
the compote
of Europe,
the Swiss
natives
hate their
aborigines

When all you needed was Manhattan

My one good year
beyond the full moon
after March, deep
and crooked,
when all you needed
was Manhattan,
the paper mill.
Its shirt is white
pulp smoke
and outside in the street
some painters and poets
running
thru the milky way of gnats,
(little gnats)
It is summer,
      12 AM
and it's raining princedom
on what was her name
at the symposium of the past.
Candide
and her blonds,
not waiting,
and the women
serving but not meeting
my eyes.
That do not seem right,
each time we touch
it is cold.
This summer
am on train
finally and
have made an
Asian soup
against hyperthermia.
the Bahnhof
is knife cold
and blood cold.
my body is
encased in cashmere
but the nose
and the butterflies
are painting painting

painting / it is
cold and I
prefer the hotel
and garden.
Our tomatoes loom
in a vapor
the white
      white
      mountains
      see the earth
      just shadows
      no one has ever touched
here with their bodies
just little animals
in the short summer season.
Say something—
I am talking—
to me.
Either OK, or nothing is
worrying me—
no mother bad or
      selfish /
Sorry, I missed your voice and
am sewing up holes
in my sweater where
lunch and dinner
were served in the
gourmet kitchen.
I am back
after the
meeting
sewing
with my nine
fingers.
The dog is a big
world now,
like the first encore
of desire
I need your talis-
man! the
work is for pleasure
kiss strong!
to the station!
      Bon Voyage!
      You are!!!

My life is
a pygmy of desire
and paint and
there are days you are
crazy / if it is
easy to leave
I heard you
laugh tonight
in the dark /
on the street
sleeping and listening
for the song
in the
dark / alone
in bed
with our talk of
a day away /
darkness
looms in the
sunshine—

On the phone

My thoughts
go back to
Jules Ferry Square
where I was given
the secrets of
unhappiness.
Anger used
itself up
and anxiety
won out as
there was no
painting or
poetry allowed
when we were
working out with
the heavy
bag.
I already
had a
shot put
in my
yard
and the
urge to
put it.
overwhelmed by the
the women
whose strength
exceeded mine,
I retreat to
the grass
to claim the
used cigarette butts.
The ring road
is easy
today and
my journey
is almost
over. The
pill is settling
my color
and I feel fine.

Jesus seems
to have come
to the kitchen
where I
work
and I ignore
all but
our Savior.
What's
to
be
done
here
beside
the addition
of some
thyme—
Paris has
metamorphosed
into
Versailles
and doesn't
know what
to do with
it.
Come with
me to the
Hotel
Oceana.
it is just
8 minutes
from the
Porte Maillot.
Green once
was all you
could see
now the
garbage
looks like
Dubuffet,
the monster.
I demand
that you
demand
a solo poem
written in the

dark.
Oh horsey
Oh blinking
red stars
that lead
us to an
urban
French
Bethlehem /
the marble
mountain
with the
gap from
being
used up
by the
Angel.
Ragged
and sore
from
too
much
friction
I go to Tokyo hands,
for a large Valise
to check thru
or get another
small one &
check all
3 thru and
try printing my heart with
many colors on what are now
black lines.
Use small
brayers or brushes
to apply ink—
Red flushed
from heat
and high blood pressure
AND paranoia,
T. Clark is killed.
The killing of the BUN man.

MURDER (for Tom Raworth)

HOPE
LOST HOPE
  with you
    and young eyes
    that are BLACK with hope
    LAST HOPE
A ghost steps out of
"PASSAGE VIVIENNE"
lower that rifle mister
the smell of glass
the smell of mosaic books
the end of traffic
    blinking at me
HEAVENLY SECRET
HEAVY WEIGHT
    of celestial
    shhhhh...
A RAGA
  Lights the sky
  with amore
  LOVE...
LOVED BY god
  AND YOU

Moscow Blue (printing in Austria 2nd version)

ABSTRACT!
LIKE THE BIG FIGURATION /
WHY NOT COMIC,
THIS CHANCE TO KILL /
SOMEONE AT RANDOM /
A TRUE (REMOTE) SIGNAL.

Late Summer, MOSCOW

i am a child with red ears
My ears are red /
A 6 year old. Pinocchio, the boy.
Down with power!!
choosing my mother, the stick becomes Jimmy
He lies down with thieves.
The stick talks thru the sand
crying since I lost /
sleeping with "bad folks"
There is an embrace
that wakes the carpenter /
i wrap my arms around my ears
and wake the cold.
My dreams, and
the red axe,
lying on the floor,
deformed by the ordinary
unusable
but my red dreams are
charged
by a cloud
that is grey.

Artemis, the last inning

I am a gene
that divides,
having had to propel
the parts
from my chest cavity
to the mantra
of the bullseye—
I practice it,
as a faith,
The soul of the target
is a journey that never
ages
The decades of
heart beats.
His contra bass
vibrates
strong anxiety. tears /
A searching portrait
of each of our mothers,
the dirty clothes
of the fathers.
Year in
year out.
It never changes.
The character of it,
never changes
and
some don't ever
feel it!
It is responsible
for grief,
Ridiculous Euphoria
and calmness.
I say forget it!
But who can dodge
the miracle
of this timeless
mystery ?
the bloodless
kickback of blood
the glowing Red
marble, the

revelation of—
finding
Elysian fields
and the song of the forest,
never again
     Le Metro /
Work the 5th step,
raise a glass
 to revenge—
but not before
retribution and
moral fairness
move us back
to Ohio in the
Autumn.
—"Oh Jewish Girls"
I drink another—
to your really
red
lips

The Way

This is the way the life begins this end of lightness
the head waits and Jesus sees some apostles with little beaded
necklaces
and no morning
cups of coffee.
i am hurting for the fool of the day
skipping the bitter meal and power
breaking the fast leg of the
heart rending news, the bias of nutrition
"don't randomize me madam"
i have lost kilos
through this trial to be free
of eggs and hunger
Lionel Messi et Janet Yellen
and four of the apostles opposing
a moody terrorist who busts up breakfast
like a child with a stick
drawing in the wet cement
portraits of the apostle
caught between this and that

Café Varenne

furiously happy,
Isaac
walks alone
in the
wilderness
thinking of
lost roses
and the new
grass to replace
tomatoes
along the
route of his
stroll.
Pull out the
bricks, my brother,
climb way
up into the
5th floor
for maids with facial hair
on the
rue des plantes.
—

the usual
greeting from
Eric is
so crazy, & now, now
subdued by the
job of
slicing
the mushroom
for
today's plat.
the memory
of those years
when your
name was
written on
the wall
and we ate
under it.
Aldo had just

come from the
Bon Marché
to give me a
carving knife.
that he felt l was
incapable of using
without his instructions.

The Bees (after Mandelstam)

For the joy in my hand,
The sun goes mad.
The bees can't fix the kisses
or the fur on the painting.
but the little bees
Are rich with their merriment.
Don't bruise the night
Send humorous presents
to the poor immigrants.
For they are the collectors of dead bees
And the eaters of their honey.

Seeing Thru the Stardust,
the Heat on the Lawn (Claude)

After Claude's death
a fair order was made of the papers.
The package of papers,
 her pleasure,
and she was in love with his voice.
Her description of me
and the time of his service
 in Strasbourg and all of Alsace,
as a son of Lorraine,
made the public aware
 of the New York connection,
AND
his idiot savant condition.
The small railway station was particular.
It was the path to melancholy.
The countryside
further heightened the
the urban quality
of the stork's nest./
You two are beautiful!
You, I put my arms around
 and nestle in your red leaves.
You are both
 Beautiful!

Dear you,
  my new bottle of ink is magic.
It draws by its tail
There are places in Havana
Where they shot at you.
The penal system there is for
brave types.
"They" are all around me,
but the chamber of dogs
fouls the new beds.
It is 6 A.M. there
and places to go,
like the levee, of
the coffee cups at home.
The underground feeling
of still being without blood.
(between my legs)

Return to the Metro!!
all the Alsatian "crybabies"
are our cousins,
(the little elves)
They pray for peace
and hope that our
time here is more
  transformative—
What a strong place!

Reveille
was good today.
I had dreamt of corn
  and other grains
To absorb my mother,
  the clowns rejoice—
There is gay laughter
  at the wake!
All at once, the
bathers scream, Yes!
When the beer and lemonade
  are served on the floor
by the fire, a pastel portrait
on 8 millimeter.
The one hundred shot glasses.
My dad
without spine, trying to
find a place in her family.
clear alcohol and these mysteries
  stand to attention.
they take the place
of sardines
and the local teenagers.
Do you understand me Mommy?
Is Daddy distributing the guns I left behind ?
Tell him the veal
  must be pounded before frying.

It is November Parisians!
Occupy the churches and
hand out the vaccine!
It will make us calm,
  hopefully
as a useful cooking utensil might.
Claude,
  the graveyard
  is a good place to study and meditate.
The views are long
  and the grass a final destination.
Just a few miles away now
  is New York.
"The porous City"
There is a white line
  thru the Celtic Sea.
What's our ground speed?
Norway; after the
consciousness of subtlety,
a drug.

The next bend in the
intestine is the appendix
  a dark creature.
Is my awareness a lie ?
How about my wakefulness?
After the important words
  become invisible,
Why can't anxiety
  be seen as an object?
Why are my eyes blind
  to the red hell?
Didn't the sun ramble?

You are my rambler
Claude.
His mother has stunning black eyebrows.
He smokes
  endlessly,
  pushing the vapor down
  and into her lungs.
She won't take her medication,
She is called "her."
Claude smokes more.
Intense
and happy in the new room
her child dances—
The city is begged to
  lower their rent.
  child is a genius
  dancer,
Tap Dancer/
  on the bridge, all the performers
  gather.

Didn't the sun ramble
Watching Claude read aloud
the letter to the folks
before he mails it?
"My life here is very
"gentile" Papa, from
an early age I have
tried to abandon ideas.
I had this lovely habit
  of being ambitious
and undervaluing failure.
I wrote my first poem.
I can't remember it. Probably
  a politic of languor.
A lion of the hanging psyche
a real apple to bite on,
not read.
No time for tragedy.

I am not sorry
  any longer
  not then
  not now,
  not real or written.
Why ?
The road of time
and the difficulty of the labor
  moves on.
What does not is wonderful
and adds pleasure
 to the clear, sad, longer
  and later private world
that my mother takes to,
under her bed.

Black eyes
Seeing thru the stardust,
The heat on the lawn
unable to come inside,
She is cold
  in the old weeds of August,
Etcetera—

The image.
A celebration of our odd behavior.
The children and the dogs
  in a corner
With the shadow
  that goes far and long
  across the paper.
A silhouette holds back
  the grape fields.
There are screams from
the Hungarian families
  as they harvest the fruit.
I have found river stones on
  the road,
    that mirror the cleft between your legs.

Now!
Blow up the brain, blow up the red risotto
  and my existence!
the alliance between us
  begins at 5 in the morning,
and continues till 3:30...
Claude was born at midnight.
He left the office at 4:45.
Cinderella forgot she
  must leave the campsite
before "Roman Night" at La Coupole.

Sunshine came across
  the grape fields today
and I betray
  my immense desire
  for your voice.
What's the manner of entry
  into the heart?
Surely not just two wires
  sent thru the arteries
  with messages
  and a liter of blood.
You, who were brought up
  to lose quarts & gallons
  now lose liters
  and in the apartment
  on 11th street
  Where went the Milanese ?

Chers Tous Deux
Dear you two...

Sometimes, I possess you

By close examination
You move the orange
   blocks over
I possess, sometimes
   But I know
   nothing
In the end is like
Printing.
It's just my eyes
   And heavy red brain
   But I have lost
Its soul
when I do laundry
   on rue Brézin.
Knowing it is near
the high desert
ear drops, we meet
   sister, brother.

Bright and Heavy

Night, I ride /
black flashing
Light objects
Become a man
        of body / but—
I cannot finish
The water.
Not there—
rocks
Snakes, Tools
Tools and stones
We always talk
room tone:
Make more room tone
slowly back to Athens
        SLOWLY

I fly down the cloud of time

I fly

Down the cloud

Of time.

My departure is unpaid for.

Not knowing what the rules

Of welcome are

I make

Myself at

Home.

We Hope

Let the hour

And the date

Fly by, with

One or two

Signs of happiness.

Amongst

The hundreds

Available.

There is

Quiet please

No choice of grub.

Who should I call

The Delta president

This guy

Should take

Some responsibility

for the lack

of ravioli on board.

No one needs

Ma anymore,

But the ducks

And their skeletons

The children are all old

With their

grandchildren.

My eyes and behind

My eyes are tired.

The ducks live

As a twosome,

Exercising their

Anatomy /

Buy radish seeds.

Plant as soon as possible.

Also Basil...

Look for more

Spice in the

New 8 x 8.

Make a device

Out of copper pipe.

Solder it

And attach to front

Of painting (of ink

Smears from

Nina's knife on paper)

Make the painting

Of high color.

Endless sleeping words

Fill the nite bladder

With verbs and zest

The snow.

Far away reminds us

      of snow as we

Know it, like a snake

On the highway.

The accelerator

Belies

Your anger and weeping.

BOB

I'm trying
to call you—
phone you—
so simple
to just pick up the phone dear speaker
Bob, dear angry guy /
dust

Johns Hopkins,
Mass General,
100 sheets
 of light.
Black Ribbon
Tiffany's
glamour sweater
Black Ribbon
 In vain
This all happened—
without calcium
Oh so recent,
the estrangement
was wary of
 Words
not that kind words
 can help—
 only
 Vitamin D.
Very useful
 To know all
this, while
sleeping,
the white robed
 Hotel
Showed up
for childhood.
adult madness
and creation.
Door is alarmed!
your black underpants
show under
the white dress
and the dimpled field.
 Goodbye
and hello!
I am to perform
everyday
so clean the aisle
 for yellow blossoms
(When) I
 see an elephant
 cry.

GAUL

france fueled
the ongoing record
of biography in
this ancient culture
based on manual
  work
and poetry / alas
he charcoaled
  himself plastic
and used everyday words
introducing the child.
Hastily assimilated
he turns to drawing.
a radical
self-assessment of
his method of
  exploring Ohio
and
the French way

Cave on the south east corner

I love the earnestness
  of mystic beauty.
in the midst of waiting
  for the voice of the Sibyl
  We fly to Vienna.
The structure of us all
  protected by will,
Auto-immune,
  or just plain anti-fascist rhetoric.
In Paris cafés,
  conversation meets the structure
  from above the wheat fields
Near the Hotel Wales,
1295 Madison Avenue

INNOCENCE

and sleep
there is a sad embrace
as we cheat the carpenter.
please wrap my arms
in white cloth
They are cold and
keep me awake
like my dreams/
I wake up/
My ears go red.
The answer

ABOUT J. Mc.

OK, MacGibbon,
to be 100% sure
  is the French way of sewing
  together my boat sails.
I refer to the quiet emotion of your loose and shining head.
An urgent moment.
I assume we have different thoughts on dancing
the sawdust on my black shirt and
The Italian obsession for worry...
is 2 images of my house
  and nation/
Go home and check on the kids. Spit on the meat
  gyrating

Last night of December

Taking place
IT EXISTS!
Blood pressure
Maria,
Laundry and all
The people
In the room.
The air sucked out by one mystery
It's called
Using your thumbs
You're always inward
The way you use your thumbs /
You know we are building a path
No one needs.
To invent usefulness by the moment,
I make enemies
With my mouth.
The great Man
makes
The words abound with
Happiness and
exclusion/
The chance
For poets and painters
In the French/
The poet sings,
he paints Red smudges,
The prophet,
For no reason.
So the man
would be loved.
I am
Grateful for
what has happened?
Anger comes up
From the feet and
My toe feels swell
compared to
whatever gets
the fools
To respect
Your queasy girlish

Nervous system/
We worry
And speak of ça va
On the subject:
You can't get a good sign from your cousins,
Mine are all gone
but one.

What a red coat!
my neck hurts.
Very crooked,
The walk into
The baroque.
The goofy right eye of Dürer,
And my memories of
Dark days
Erased by distance.
The barley risotto
In my kitchen makes people
feel silly and stupid
(are you ok?)
I'm only waiting
For your happiness
(yeah, yeah, we know)
it seemed the year was very cheery,
With a lightness of body

Matt Strucktur-Gel

Title for
The big head.
Horace and Ovid

Horace meets Ovid ?
your singing so clear,
so pure, so simple.
A painting echo
Lives in the
dance.
The early nought,
jump on the back
To reach the top
for 30 years we work
And get nothing.
My brother
says hello.

Elysian Fields

and the song of the forest—
never again the Métro so work the fifth step
and raise a glass to revenge
to reneging
to relishing and to fascism,
a word that now walks in
but not before retribution
and moral fairness
moves us back to Ohio in the autumn/
O Canada
I drink another to your really full red lips
and—
to the Champs Élysées (that's French for Elysian (Fields) which is
why I titled the poem that)

MY MEMORY

when radar
ends the errant rays,
a constant reminder
of eternal life.
The ocean remains at home
as seeds escape the memory of eternal life
young roses
shoot red buds now
that winterkill is pale
it is necessary
to be robust,
when the radar ends
the errant rays,
seeds escape the ocean
what stays at home with
the roses
as she shoots her red buds...
winter kills the paleness
its really necessary to be robust
a constant reminder of eternal life.
Who cares?
about this movement of tranquility
Take it—
Have a sandwich
grab a drink, a hotdog
Sing about the days of March
resign and mourn
as losses remain stable.
The tunes of a badger
The brusk notes
The discord of his D key.
now don't do anything rash,
remember we all come from good families

It ends at Seattle

so i wonder i stand up
and wed my tomatoes
and once the world
views the host and my weeds
Why did this garden come this Monday?
I'm being disagreeable
Come on Japan
Lower the voice,
bring green to the leaves,
smile like a moron

A Song at Twilight
for Tom Raworth in palliative care

The work is exciting—
the bean sprouts, about the Thai basil,
Weak
He's weak
Hemoglobin low, weak
The Essex poet sends me
More, on this godlike morning sperm.
Sperm,
this morning the last 3 colors came like sperm
innocent and boyish the Poët Laval awaits my charm and beauty
the bahnhof is full of beggars
The Pho is swell
send me more
like the last 3 colors
arriving like morning sperm.
An innocent young boy and the Poët Laval,
Paris awaits them and my charm
Pho is very hot!
The bahnhof is full of gypsies.

2017

An old child wanders
during the roman sunshine
in January I wonder
at the tomb of San Luca
I know my years,
as the skin, bunching like
my sweater arms,
folds like a paper
wrapper on the flesh,
fresh from the cupboard
and alive
like Velcro
The sun
looks gold on the forum

For Ron, in Calais

The mode
 of falling evening
Wrings the hands of
 this old Ranger
How dreadful the truth can be,
When there's no help
 for the tired man
When all this is ok/
 watch out for the rabid
 dogs now...
How awful the truth can be
 when looking for our moral lives
 I'm danger one day,
 who knows
This family
 and the passion
The singular loneliness
Our very own blood (or bones)
 so different—
 like red or yellow or blue
 explosions—
 that scarred the grass
 or as we then called it—
 the vacant lot

Pinocchio's room

More discreet
less shining,
more
pigment
on the boy /
have to make
a date for
a night
of fine glass.
The paint
that lags
beneath the tragic /
a lost factory
of error.

Meeting of the carvers

Jim finally
is ill equipt
to deal
with the competitive
world
of puppets,
the tranquility of Tuscan politics,
cares, and the business
of life.
Greek temples
at Paestum
Geppetto at Pompei
magnificence
followed by
inevitable decline

photograph by Daniel Clarke
Málaga, Spain June 2019

MY POETRY BIOGRAPHY

I was born in 1935. The real story is that I didn't meet poetry till I was nineteen when my sculpture professor, Dave Hosteller, at Ohio University, played Dylan Thomas reading his poems an a Caedmon 'LP' record. He also gave me *Under Milk Wood* (Thomas' radio play) to listen to.

During my early twenties, I made performances in New York with colleagues in the 'downtown' art world. My most elaborate work, called *Car Crash,* was a cacophony of sounds and words spoken by a great white Venus with animal grunts and howls by me. Five years later, I illustrated Ron Padgett's translation of Apollinaire's *The Poet Assassinated.* Meeting Ron introduced me to his work and the works of other poets he admired. At the same time, I met and fell in love with Robert Creeley. He was, to me, all about poetry. He was generous with his thoughts, but it was his Massachusetts-accented voice that was the poetry. I read Ted Berrigan's *The Sonnets.* It was 1966, and I started to write poetry full force around then.

I went to England in 1967 and met the poet-printers Asa Benveniste and Tom Raworth. Asa wanted to publish my poems. He did. The book was called *Welcome Home Lovebirds*. There were a lot of letters and postcards written between me and U.S. poets. In London, there was much talk around Asa about poetry and Asa's history as a poet and publisher of poets. He was, I guess, ten years older than me.

I started to write every day and continued till about 1972 when I stopped. I'm not clear why, but I began again around 1990 when I met Diana Michener. She is a very inspirational character, and her eccentric big soul understands all I've written since. We have read together in public with the New York poet, Vincent Katz, who has befriended my poems. I have learned from his personal vision.

Many of my poems are written first on long sheets of paper tacked to the wall. Some are eight or nine feet long, and I write in charcoal or crayon and then 'white out' when I want to change a word, with a mixture of white pigment mixed with shellac. I also can cut out a line with a box cutter and lose it or use it in another place in the poem by gluing it or stapling it to the paper on the wall. This technique is a lot like the way I draw. Correcting and erasing are important tools, for my poems *and* my drawings.

— Jim Dine, 2020

A Song at Twilight was edited by Vincent Katz
designed by Jim Dine & Kyle Schlesinger
& typeset in Martin Majoor's Scala
there are 500 copies of this first
edition of which 26 are
lettered & signed by
the author

·

Some of the poems included in this book were first published in: *Envelope*; *Jewish Fate* (Steidl, 2018); *My Letter to the Troops* (Steidl, 2018); *Nantes* (éditions joca seria, 2017); *La Coupole et autres poèms* (éditions joca seria, 2017); *Paris Reconnaissance* (Steidl, 2018); *Seeing Thru the Stardust, the Heat on the Lawn (Claude)* (Jardin des Tuileries, 2017). Special thanks to Olivier Brossard, Vincent Broqua, Daniel Clarke, Abigail Lang, & Beatrice Trotignon.